101

WAYS TO WORK WITH AN ASSHOLE

(AND SUCCEED ANYWAY!)

LOU HARRY

CIDER MILL PRESS

BOOK PUBLISHERS

KENNEBUNKPORT, MAINE

13-Digit ISBN: 978-1-60433-741-9
10-Digit ISBN: 1-60433-741-9

This book may be ordered by mail from the
publisher. Please include $5.99 for postage and
handling. Please support your local bookseller
first!

Books published by Cider Mill Press Book
Publishers are available at special discounts
for bulk purchases in the United States
by corporations, institutions, and other
organizations. For more information, please
contact the publisher.

Cider Mill Press Book Publishers
"Where good books are ready for press"
PO Box 454
12 Spring Street
Kennebunkport, Maine 04046

Visit us on the Web! www.cidermillpress.com

Cover design by Jon Chaiet
Interior design by Abigail Spooner
Illustrations by Alex Kalomeris
Typography: Garamond Premier Pro & Gotham

Printed in the United States
1 2 3 4 5 6 7 8 9 0
First Edition

Contents

Introduction

ASSHOLE COWORKERS COME in all shapes and sizes.

Even when the discussion is limited to assholes at the workplace, there's a wide range, from the ones that won't get out of your face to the ones who do everything behind your back. There's the blowhard boss, the take-credit-for-everything coworker, the buck-passer, and, well, no doubt you've compiled your own list during your work life.

Because of their seemingly infinite variety, there's not a single solution to dealing with all assholes. In this book, you'll find 101 ways of dealing with an office asshole.

Some of them may seem contradictory, but the truth is that some methods work on some assholes. Some on others.

In some circumstances, you may need to combine techniques for maximum effectiveness. In others, a single approach could work.

Whatever the case, know that we've all been there.

And that you have our sympathies.

Good luck.

The Evolution of the Asshole

Report Him/Her

SINCE OUR YOUNGEST days, we are inundated with the message that tattling on someone is wrong. But remember that telling your boss about something that is impacting happiness and/or productivity in the workplace isn't the same as ratting out a friend to the House of Un-American Activities Committee. If your boss doesn't know about the asshole's behavior, the boss can't really do anything about it, right? Just make sure before you do that the boss isn't already firmly in the asshole's corner.

Suggest a Promotion

THIS ONE MIGHT be a bit hard to stomach, but if you can help orchestrate a promotion (preferably to a different venue) for the asshole, they'll be out of your hair — at least until you get promoted to the same spot. Plant those seeds carefully, though, lest it becomes clear that you are being motivated by self-interest rather than the good of the company.

Get on Good Side

THERE'S A FINE line between capitulation and getting on an asshole's good side. Whether you are in your workplace for the long haul or simply need to buy some time while you plan a drastic move, getting on the asshole's good side can make life much easier. Proceed cautiously, though. Taking this approach can do damage to your pride — and make sure your fellow victimized employees don't feel like you've gone over to the dark side.

Baked Goods

IT IS COMMON knowledge that brownies and other baked goods actually earn brownie points (hence the name) in a wide range of workplace environments. And knowing the asshole's calorie-packed preference is helpful. The problem is that the asshole may not even know that you are the one supplying the goods. Even worse, they may figure you are buttering up the whole department rather than doing something just for them. Making it obvious that you are doing it just for them, however, may come across as a little creepy, so consider yourself warned!

Blame the Source

THE ASSHOLE DIDN'T give themselves the job. The asshole was hired. So, assuming they didn't evolve into their assholeness, that means that part of the blame for your office nightmare should rest firmly in the human resources department. Chumming up to HR, finding out what the standards really are, and helping develop new criteria for hiring may not help you deal with your current asshole, but could help future ones from entering the workplace pipeline.

Remember,
Assholes Can Be Effective

NOBODY IS ASKING you to excuse bad behavior, but the unfortunate reality is that assholes can actually do a good job sometimes. And it's essential to understand that before you prepare to wage war. Who's the greatest secret agent in literature? James Bond, right? Well, in the Bond novel *Casino Royale*, he has this to say about women: "Why couldn't they stay at home and mind their pots and pans and stick to their frocks and gossip and leave men's work to me?" If that isn't an asshole, I don't know what is. Assessing the office asshole's actual effectiveness is a key step in plotting a strategy to deal with them.

Own Your Ideas

IT'S NOT UNCOMMON for an office asshole to claim other people's ideas as their own. How do you prevent such intellectual plagiarism? Make sure that there are witnesses to your ideas before the asshole gets wind of them. Giving away a few key elements to the boss before the big reveal will not only protect your ideas but will also force a joyfully awkward moment when the asshole tries to take credit for an idea that is already known to be yours.

№ 8

Look to the Future

TODAY, YOU'VE GOT a problem. But there's always tomorrow. Make sure that, whatever your course of action, you think through not just what your action will mean today, but what it will mean next week, next month, and next year. Similarly, thinking about the weekend or vacation ahead could help get you through the rough patch today.

Shut Up (for now)

NO, KEEPING QUIET isn't usually the smartest thing in the long run. But in the short term, quietly assessing a situation — especially if you are a relative newcomer to the job — may be wise. Make observational notes. Scribble down questions you may eventually want answered.
But hold your tongue until you have a fuller grasp of the situation and the players.

Threaten to Quit

THIS ONE CAN backfire unless you actually plan on cutting the cord if the ploy doesn't work. But when push comes to shove — and you want to try one last thing before you push yourself out the door — letting your boss know that you've reached your limit and it's either them or you might be the Hail Mary pass that both saves your job and gets rid of them. It helps increase your odds, of course, if by this time you've made yourself as indispensable as possible to the company.

Quit

IT'S DRASTIC, YES, but if the workplace has become too toxic, sometimes getting out is the best strategy. But unless you are a recent lottery winner or have a partner with a nice run of digits in their paycheck, this is a move you must plan, not one you just jump into. A dramatic "I quit" scene in your boss' office, featuring finger-pointing at the offending asshole, may make for a satisfying movie scene, but it can lead to intense remorse the day after.

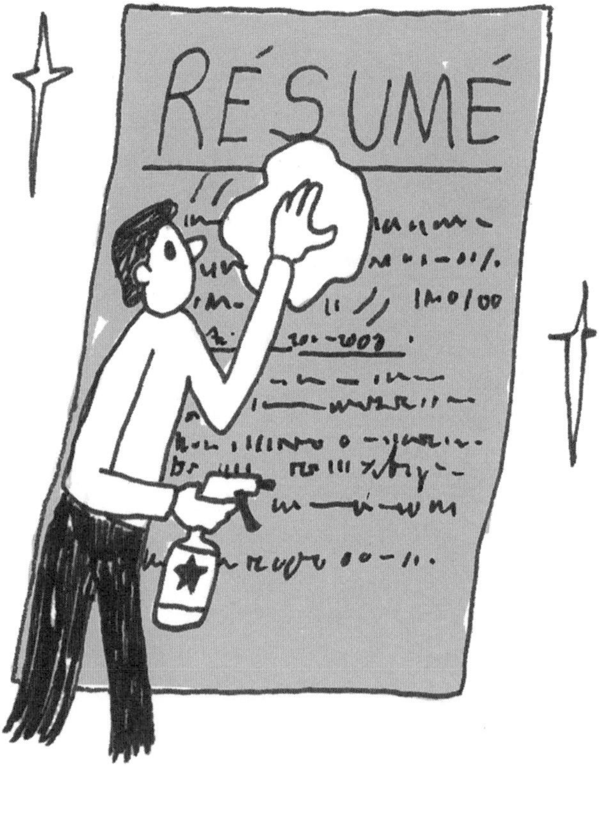
RÉSUMÉ

№ 12

Polish the Résumé

IF YOU ARE planning on exiting your job, getting your résumé in shape is mandatory. But even if you aren't going to make the leap, cleaning up the résumé can serve a purpose, helping remind you that there are other options for someone as bright and talented and hardworking as yourself. And that knowledge could empower you to deal more directly with the asshole at hand, in a way that could actually solidify your current gig.

Notify Headhunters

WHY NOT HAVE a team doing some of the job-hunting work for you? In many jobs, getting your credentials in front of job headhunters could help you discover opportunities you never knew existed. Fielding offers feels great and, even if these next-step options are less than ideal, their existence could put you in a better bargaining position when you have that closed door meeting with your boss.

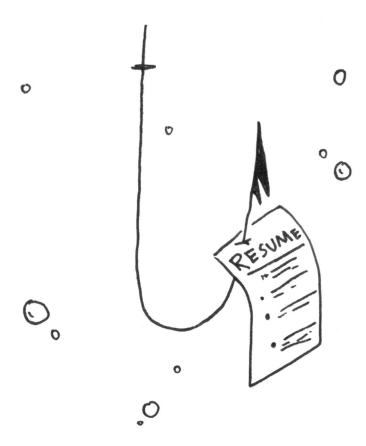

Diplomacy

OFFICE POLITICS CAN be just that — politics. And contrary to how some elected officials may act, diplomacy is a key element in being politically effective. So exercise those skills — or try them out for the first time — by treating the asshole like a congressperson from across the aisle whose vote you need on an important bill.

Assess Your Own Biases

AT THE RISK of putting you on the defensive, there's a chance…a small chance, but a chance nonetheless…that your biases may be influencing your assessment of your coworker. Before you turn the page, keep in mind that we all have biases. We're human. And being aware of our biases and how they may be manifesting can go a long way toward defusing conflict.

Review Harassment Policy

THERE COMES A point where assholeness crosses over into harassment. That's why you should have a clear understanding of your office's harassment policies, even before experiencing the first sign of asshole behavior. You might be surprised to find that the asshole is already in clear violation of written policy, which will make it easier to take decisive action.

Listen

WHEN THERE'S AN asshole around, it's easy to assume that everything they say falls under that asshole umbrella. But as the saying goes, even a broken clock is right twice a day. Disregard everything the asshole says and you run the risk of seeming like an asshole yourself. To avoid that, assess each encounter or edict from the asshole on its own merits. In other words, don't always consider the source.

Avoid Complaining on Social Media

WE SOMETIMES LIKE to believe that our Facebook and Instagram pages, Twitter feeds, etc. are private little worlds where we communicate with our friends and family who have nothing but our best interests at heart. But, of course, that's not the case. Post something on your social media wall and you might as well be broadcasting it on radio, running an ad in your local newspaper, and hanging a sign on your front door. Post your complaints about your coworker and you can be sure that it's going to be used against you.

Out-asshole the Asshole

IF YOU CAN'T beat 'em, well, maybe you aren't trying hard enough. Fighting fire with fire has a long history and, occasionally, it works. But remember that any asshole retaliation could be used against you once you start upping the asshole arms race. You could find yourself on the receiving end of a pink slip if your assholeness takes on a higher profile than your rival's.

Don't Let Them Get to You

YEAH. YEAH. EASIER said than done. But unless the asshole that's making your life miserable is the head of the company and there's no chain-of-command buffer between them and you, remind yourself that you do have some breathing room, that it's not healthy for you to let them define your office life, and that letting them get to you is letting them win.

Document

IF IT COMES to reporting your workplace asshole to HR or to your supervisor, your story is going to carry a lot more weight if you have documentation to back up the offending incidents.   Writing in the moment with as much detail as possible not only helps discern patterns, it also helps keep your memory from embellishing, which could leave your story open to questions. Save the file on a personal computer, not just on the one at work.

Assess Their Expectations

SOMETIMES WE LABEL someone an asshole because of the expectations they put on us. (What child among us hasn't muttered similar things about his parents under his breath?) Ask yourself if you are hostile toward the alleged asshole because they're expecting more of you than you are comfortably willing to do. The challenge, then, is to rise to the occasion rather than throw blame.

Avoid / Limit Contact

SOMETIMES, WHEN THERE'S conflict with a coworker, your brain may tell you to stay away but you still may feel drawn to the asshole, subconsciously trying to provoke them into more overt acts of assholeness. Being aware of that impulse may help you avoid giving in to it. With an asshole at large, it's best to minimize contact without compromising the quality of your work. And by all means, stay away from one-on-one encounters sans witnesses.

Isolate

KEEPING AN ASSHOLE at arm's length is important, and you can make that arm longer by making sure not to include the asshole when you gather coworkers for a lunch excursion or a closing-time drink at the local watering hole. Sending a consistent message that being an asshole leads to pariah status may help modify the behavior. If nothing else, it could give you a haven for at least some of your precious time.

Explore the Backstory

BEHIND EVERY ASSHOLE there is, well, who knows? But who we were impacts who we are, so it may be worth checking into the backstory of your office asshole. You may find clues that provide an insight that might help you deal with the asshole...or perhaps even sympathize a bit with the circumstances that made them the asshole they are today. That's not saying our history excuses our bad behavior. It's just that context can feed your strategy for coping.

Keep Your Eyes on the Prize

NOT EVERYONE WE work with is, officially, a coworker. We often have to deal with clients, representatives of other businesses, and, of course, customers. When those assholes enter your workspace, your options are significantly more limited. In those cases, it's helpful to keep an eye on the prize, reminding yourself of the positive impact of the asshole on your business, whether that's direct (a sale today) or indirect (a gateway to an important business connection).

Get It in Writing

IF THAT JERK client is the kind of asshole who keeps changing the rules on you, learn from the past. Get all future agreements, assignments or deals in writing. If nothing else, have an agreed upon checklist that you can (figuratively) throw in their face the next time they act like you didn't live up to your end of the bargain.

Meltdown

JUST ASK ANYONE who works in commercial real estate: Sometimes you need to break down before you can build up to something stronger. When it comes to the workplace, that doesn't mean you should have a temper tantrum or a public crying jag at the slightest provocation. But a private meltdown can be rejuvenating, helping you let out pent-up feelings rather than build up to an explosion later.

Mockery

YES, TURNING THE office asshole into an object of ridicule is juvenile. But that doesn't mean it can't be invigorating. Finding an obvious character trait of the asshole and exaggerating it to comic effect can be a fun release if — and this is a big IF — you have a coworker that you can trust not to ever let it get back to the asshole in question or to a supervisor.

Camaraderie with Coworkers

OFFICE CAMARADERIE DOESN'T mean rounding up support like the whip in Congress. It may not even matter if they are on your side or even realize that the asshole is, in fact, an asshole. The point here is that an occasional reminder that the workplace isn't just you and the asshole can help make your unpleasant dealings easier. Take advantage of social opportunities. Engage in small talk. Find opportunities to make or solidify those connections.

Take to Lunch / Coffee

IT MAY END up being the most awkward hour of your work life, but taking the office asshole out to lunch or even just a cup of coffee could be a step toward breaking the ice. It's helpful to go in prepared, so have some conversation starters to get things rolling, avoid talking directly about the conflict — unless they bring it up — and strap yourself in for the duration. Familiarity isn't guaranteed to reduce assholeness, but it can begin to build a bridge.

Talk to Your Union Rep

OF COURSE, THIS is irrelevant if you are not part of a labor union. But if you are, remember that wages and benefits aren't the only thing that your union is there for. It's also there to make sure that you are working in a safe, fair, and productive environment. They are also there to protect you if there's any backlash from reporting the asshole's actions.

Don't Assume

WHEN YOU EXPERIENCE someone blatantly treating you and others like crap, it's easy to assume that the asshole knows that they're an asshole. But as any good fiction writer will tell you, villains rarely think of themselves as villains. They are just the entitled heroes of their own stories. Approaching the asshole as if they're deliberately trying to be the bad guy can be less productive than seeing what they are trying to achieve and why they might think those means are worth the projected ends.

Install Company Values

SOME COMPANIES HAVE a mission statement or statement of values that clearly defines what is and isn't acceptable for anyone working at the company. Many others have murky mission statements that really only say that a long committee meeting was wasted coming up with the most innocuous, generic terminology possible. Still other companies, particularly smaller businesses, have no such mission statement at all. If your company is one of the latter, you can propose helping draft such a statement with your bosses. Include values that clearly aren't being demonstrated by the office asshole.

Hide Behind the Work

WHETHER IT'S ACTUALLY hiding or just temporarily retreating to a place where you can actually be productive while wallowing in your misery, burying yourself in your to-do list can keep you from digging a deeper hole. You don't want to have to deal with the asshole AND supervisors who have noted that your output has dropped off recently. When that meeting happens, blaming the asshole can come across as just passing the buck.

Get a Witness

ARE YOUR COWORKERS aware of the asshole's behavior toward you? If not, the stories you tell later may come across as paranoid ramblings. You need someone who is going to be able to corroborate your observations or, at least, provide comfort and moral support in your efforts to endure. It can be even more useful if this witness isn't someone who is well-known to be your office buddy. That quiet person in the cubicle on the end may be the most impartial — and ultimately impressive and trusted — witness.

Laugh

THE CLICHÉ THAT laughter is the best medicine may be overstating the case a bit, but a good chuckle can often diffuse a situation. It can give an asshole an opportunity to back off a minor infraction and, at the same time, can show how above it all you are. Scott Adams, of Dilbert fame, made his career out of finding humor in office headaches. If you don't have a reliably laugh-inducing coworker, keep a list of go-to funny websites, whether that's the cartoon page of the *New Yorker* or a page of funny memes. Remember: These aren't jokes to impress others, just places that you know can reliably tickle your funny bone when desperately needed.

Connect the Jerkiness to Job Performance

THIS ONE ISN'T going to be easy, but rather than take the asshole's approach as an insult, take a serious look at whether or not your own job performance is impacting the degree of assholeness being lobbed in your direction. That by no means is an excuse for bad behavior, but if you are the only one in the office being targeted — and if you are the only one who thinks that the asshole is actually an asshole — then take a look at your own productivity.

Request an Evaluation or Annual Review

IF YOUR WORKPLACE isn't one where you are regularly informed about how you are or aren't meeting overall expectations, it can be difficult to know if the asshole is isolated in their attitude toward you or if the problem is wider. Knowledge can be an uncomfortable thing, but it's usually best to know where you stand. Request an evaluation or annual review with your supervisor. If this is already part of the office routine, try to objectively hear what's being said the next time one rolls around. A positive review can also remind you that the problem isn't with you. Even if you already knew that, it's nice to have that reinforcement.

Count Small Victories

WHILE YOU BIDE your time and plan for the big victory — which boils down to either the asshole leaving, you leaving, or the asshole changing their ways — try counting the small victories that make you a better person and a better employee than the asshole. Keep a file of kind words and positive reports about your work. Compile and continue to build a list of the things you've done that have directly had a positive impact on your workplace, even if they haven't been acknowledged or appreciated by others. Do this not just to increase your value at work, but to remind yourself of how valuable you truly are.

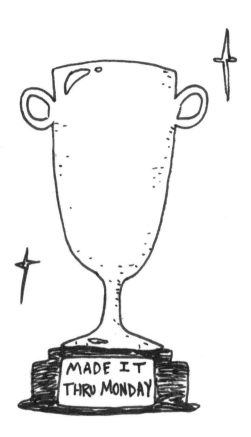

Find Fellow Victims

IF THE ASSHOLE is truly an asshole, there's a good chance that they haven't just singled you out. Watch how they behaves around your coworkers. Touch base with former coworkers who have moved on. If you can find a pattern, consider presenting a united front to your supervisor —provided the asshole isn't your supervisor's cousin. Which leads to...

Find out How the Asshole Was Hired

KNOWING THE CIRCUMSTANCES that brought the asshole into the company could go a long way toward figuring out how to deal with them. Was there nepotism involved? Does the asshole have a specific, desirable skill that would be difficult to replace? Do they have seniority or political pull? Who specifically did they impress enough to be offered a job? Of course, this is easier with recent hires and certainly easier said than done with those who have been around far longer than you.

Request Reassignment

GETTING AWAY FROM an asshole doesn't have to mean finding a new company to work for. If your company is big enough, a request for reassignment — even down the hall — could give you enough space to get you back up to full functionality. Make sure, though, the move is something you might have requested anyway so that your motives aren't questioned. And remind your boss how much you love working for them despite the asshole.

Legal Action

WHEN THE BEHAVIOR of the office asshole crosses the line from casual to criminal — or when the higher-ups in your company turn deaf ears to your reasonable concerns about behavior that should warrant, at best, firing — then it could be time to connect with a lawyer. And with approximately 40,000 law degrees being passed out annually, there should be no shortage of lawyers out there willing to consider your case.

Educate the Asshole

BEING AN ASSHOLE can be a thinly veiled way to avoid admitting that you aren't as bright or knowledgeable as you need to be to successfully carry out your job. By acting out, the asshole keeps people from looking at the quality of their work. If that seems to be the case, educating the asshole could help. Take on the task of subtly helping to bring the asshole up to speed without letting on your ulterior motive.

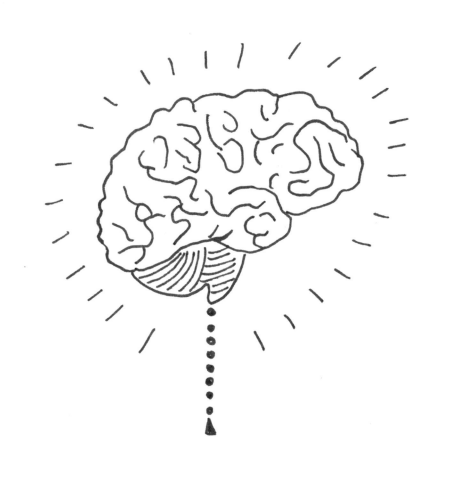

Push for More Training

THERE ARE TIMES when, as in the previous suggestion, the office asshole really just needs some education. But you can't always do that by yourself. Encouraging your workplace to focus more directly on specific deficits in the asshole's experience not only could help the current situation, but could also be a preventative strike against future assholes.

Embrace the Lack of Change

THE FAMOUS WORDS of Alcoholics Anonymous encourage members to accept the things one cannot change. And it's highly possible that the office asshole could be one of those things in life that cannot be changed. If other methods have been exhausted, you may find yourself in the position of having to accept that — at least until you are ready to find another place to work.

Take It Home

IT'S EASY — and often destructive — to act in the moment. If you're lucky, though, you have a team of advisors on the home front. That could be a partner, a parent, or an overeducated college grad child still living in the house. Whatever the case, bouncing the office circumstances off someone who can at least pretend impartiality could give you the distance you need to assess whether true assholery is actually going on.

Leave It at the Office

ON THE OTHER hand, leaving the negative vibes at the office may prove to be the better option. Just because your office place is poison doesn't mean you have to spread it to the home front. Keep a safe space at home where you can focus on other things that help let some of the air out of the about-to-burst balloon of office life.

Pray

PUTTING ASIDE WHETHER or not there actually is a God who intervenes in human affairs, there still can be a benefit to prayer. Like meditation, purposeful prayer can help clear some of the clutter that's keeping you from being able to focus on what you can and can't impact. It can help you strategize for the greater good, not just for what seems like it might be best for you. And it can help you find peace, forgiveness, or both.

№ 51

Non-Verbal Messaging

THERE ARE WAYS to send a message that you aren't happy with an asshole's behavior that are subtler than a screaming match. Close the door on them when they are raising their voice on the phone. Avoid eye contact when they're monopolizing a meeting. Pretend you don't hear them when they call to you from across the office. Small victories can add up.

Don't Buy In

IF THE OFFICE asshole is also the office gossip, it can be tempting to buy into their behavior...provided they're sharing dirt on someone else. Even when the news seems particularly juicy, avoid buying into the gossip game. Remember that the asshole's gossip could be sharing information —accurate or not — about you next time.

Chill before Confronting or Reporting

IF YOU ARE going to confront the asshole or report them to a supervisor, try not to do it in the heat of a recent infraction. Give yourself the time to distance yourself a bit from the emotion of the moment and to collect your thoughts so that you come across as the sane one in the conflict.

SELF AWARENESS

Make Them Self-aware

SOMETIMES, CALLING IT like you see it can be like a cold washcloth on the face of the asshole, waking them up to reality. Call out the asshole behavior in a concise, matter-of-fact way. Just remember to focus on the behavior rather than slap on a label. "You're behaving like an asshole" is better than "You are an asshole."

Self-reflect

IS THE ASSHOLE focusing their attention on you? Do they seem to get along fine and treat everyone fairly except you? Then some self-reflection should be in order. Trying to determine if there's something about you that's drawing such unwarranted attention doesn't mean the action is your fault or that the asshole is innocent. But it's worth analyzing if something you are doing is serving as a trigger.

Give a Second (or Fifth) Chance

WE'VE ALL STUMBLED at our workplaces at one time or another. And we hope that others aren't judging us by that misstep. So while asshole behavior is asshole behavior, there's a chance that the incident that ticked you off is an anomaly. Giving a second chance — or perhaps more — will either solidify your workmate's asshole standing or make clear that the good (or, at least, the acceptable) outweighs the bad.

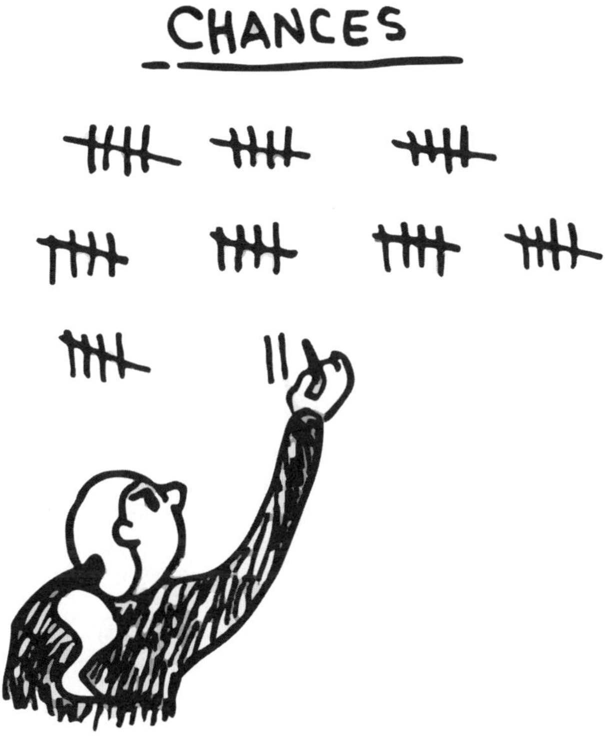
CHANCES

Avoid Encounters

THIS ISN'T A suggestion that you hide under your desk whenever the asshole is around or sneak out through the fire exit at the end of the day. But it is a suggestion that you minimize encounters with the offending jerk. The fewer extraneous encounters, the lower the potential for volatility.

...Especially on Friday

UNLESS YOU ARE firing someone, Friday is the worst time for office confrontation. Why? Because there's a good chance that whatever gets brought up isn't going to be resolved by the end of the workday. And that means you are heading into a very frustrating weekend where hostilities can fester and nothing much can be done to mitigate the mess.

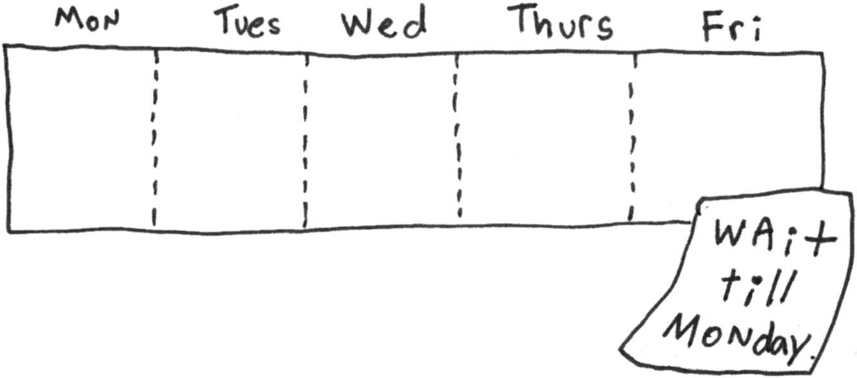
Mon
Tues
Wed
Thurs
Fri
WAit till Monday.

Prank 1: The Keyboard

GRAB A FLATHEAD screwdriver and do a rearrangement on the asshole's keyboard. If they're a decent typist, they might not notice the letter keys, so best to mess with the ones that require even the best typist to peek down. Of course, if you're even slightly tech savvy, you can leave the tool at home and, instead, simply reassign the keys.

Prank 2: Growth Industry

STILL HAVE THAT Chia pet you were given at the last office white elephant gift exchange? Well, if you haven't already planted the seeds — and have some patience for a gag to pay off — pay a clandestine visit to the asshole's computer, tuck the wet seeds deeply between the keys where they won't be seen, and wait for nature to take its course.

Prank 3: Autocorrect Reset

THE DETAILS ARE different depending on the software you use, but the result is the same: Frustration for the asshole. Just reset their autocorrect function to change a commonly used word around your office — or just the asshole's name — into something different. Think of the fun when, every time they type their own name, it's replaced with "Asshole McJerkface."

Prank 4: Mouse Magic

THIS ONE'S SIMPLE. And simply effective. You'll need access to their laser mouse (assuming they use one, if not, turn the page). All you have to do is tape over the laser spot and color over the tape with a black marker. Voilà: A not-functioning mouse that will cause at least a few minutes of frustration for them and bliss for you while they shake and bang it.

Prank 5: Help Wanted

TRACK DOWN THE asshole's job description. Submit it — again, through a computer not your own — onto as many employment sites as you can find — and make sure to give the asshole's phone number and email address as the person to contact. Maybe they'll take a hint and their job will soon actually be available.

Prank 6: Freezer Follies

IF YOUR ASSHOLE coworker brings their own pre-packaged box lunches, wait until they're safely away from the breakroom, sneak in, and write your boss' name, with marker, on them. Come lunchtime, the asshole will find themselves on the uncertain side and you can watch with pleasure as they wrestle with whether or not to take the chance and steal the boss' food.

Prank 7:
E-mail Clogging

THEY'VE GOT AN e-mail address. And thousands of companies would love to have it. If you're in a revenge mood that doesn't do any physical harm, wouldn't it be fun to spend an afternoon at the public library — or at another computer not your own — getting them registered on all sorts of fun and/or bizarre e-mail lists?

Make the Business Case against Jerks

NO MATTER HOW much you've been wronged, some employers will show little or no interest in making things right. Unless, of course, it impacts the company profits. If you can build a case that the office asshole's behavior is making the business look bad to customers or clients, keeping desirable talent from joining the company, or otherwise negatively influencing the bottom line, you may be able to win this battle peacefully.

Avoid E-mail

IT CAN BE tempting to fire off a note while you are still raging about the behavior of the workplace asshole. Resist this temptation. You don't want to leave a paper trail unless you are in a completely clear, purposeful mind and understand how what you write can work for or against you. If you e-mail it, consider it available to the public. You don't want that.

Assess Your Circle of Influence

WHEN SOMEONE ELSE is behaving like an asshole, it's easy to believe that they're in complete control of the situation and, thus, dominate the workplace. It's important when such feelings hit to step back and take an honest look at what your sphere of influence actually consists of. Knowing where your own power lies can help you get a more realistic view of the power games being played.

Address in Private

RATHER THAN MAKE a public scene of it, consider addressing the matter privately with the asshole. Take "consider" seriously here because what you don't want is a volatile situation without witnesses. But if the asshole behavior seems like it could be manageable, a bit of one-on-one may help eliminate the behavior if handled in a non-confrontational, "let's clear the air" way.

Turn the Other Cheek

THIS ONE MAY be one of the toughest. But it is one prescribed in the New Testament. It's right there in the book of Matthew. Chapter 5, verse 39, to be specific. Translations vary, but the *King James Bible* offers it as: "whosoever shall smite thee on thy right cheek, turn to him the other also."

Agree to Disagree

STANDING UP TO an office bully doesn't have to have the goal of getting rid of them. And accepting that things may not change doesn't have to mean staying silent. Make clear to the asshole that you know they're an asshole and that both of you are just going to have to deal with each other.

Avoid Labels

SAYING SOMEONE DID something asinine or is acting like a jerk is different than saying that the person is an asshole or a jerk. One is a description of behavior and the other is a label. Someone who behaves like an asshole can behave differently in your mind. But once you slap an asshole label on someone, that's going to be hard to shake. Avoiding labels gives you a psychological way out.

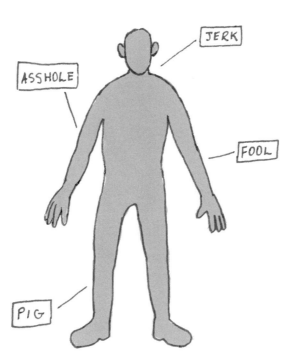

Gravitate to the Good Folks

THE MORE YOU obsess on the behavior of the asshole, the less time you may be spending cultivating relationships with the good people at your workplace. And when it comes down to it, the power of one asshole is severely reduced when you've got the right allies in your corner. That doesn't have to mean building an army against the asshole. It simply means gravitating toward what's healthy rather than focusing on the unhealthy.

Focus on the Problem Rather Than the Person

YES, YOU HAVE reason to be pissed off at the person who is being an asshole. But, more specifically, there's a specific asshole action of that person that's making your life miserable. By focusing on the problem rather than the person, you've got a more manageable target — one with an easier-to-identify set of potential solutions.

Therapy

REAL LIFE CAN be overwhelming. But before it overwhelms you, consider seeking professional help. There's no shame in seeking the help of a professional therapist — and your insurance may well cover at least a part of it. A good therapist will listen and help guide you toward decisions that are healthy and productive.

Look for Triggers

JUST AS A good poker player looks for "tells," you can look for actions that seem to trigger the office asshole's asshole behavior. Do they get pissy just days before the paychecks arrive? Does the jerkiness escalate when the pressure is highest? Or does the behavior seem to manifest more often when there's less to do? It could be that things get worse when the boss is out of town. Spotting such triggers can help you bob and weave your way out of the line of hellfire.

Confuse the Asshole

THIS CAN BE as minor as tossing the occasional nonsequitur into conversation or it can be full-on gaslighting where your random acts lead the asshole to confusion and self-doubt. Speak French but the asshole doesn't? Drop a little randomly into your private conversations, pretending that it never happened when they point it out. Leave notes (untraceable to you) about meetings that actually aren't going to happen. Periodically take away all of the pens on their desk. If nothing else, you'll amuse yourself coming up with the next odd action.

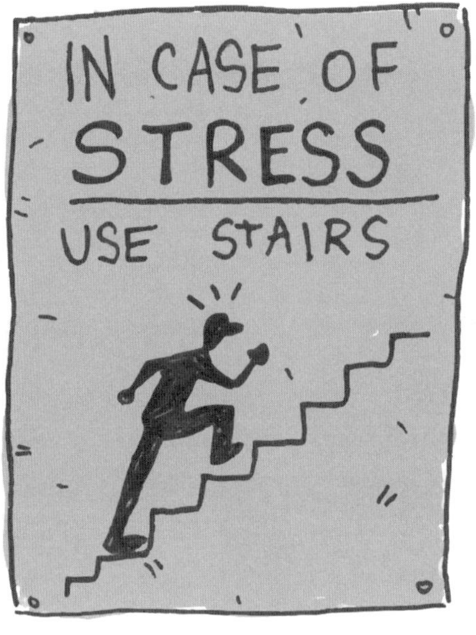
IN CASE OF
STRESS
USE STAIRS

Walkabout

IT DOESN'T MATTER if your workplace has its own gym, if it's housed in some cookie-cutter suburban office park, or if you're on the 39th floor of a big-city highrise — there's going to be some place for you to walk off some of your frustration and built-up aggression. A visit to the elliptical, a lap around the retention pond, or a trek up and down the staircases can take the edge off.

Read your Machiavelli

"IT IS BETTER to be feared than loved if you cannot be both," wrote Niccolo Machiavelli, the Italian Renaissance writer often cited for his cutthroat approach to political relationships. Business leaders before you have mined his book, *The Prince*, for guidance and it's certainly worth a look for such gems as, "Wisdom consists of knowing how to distinguish the nature of trouble, and in choosing the lesser evil."

Emotionally Detach

A FANCY WAY of saying "not caring," "emotionally detaching" doesn't mean becoming an unfeeling automaton. It means not expending precious emotional energy on a situation of which you have little control. Avoiding an emotional reaction — whether that's hurt, annoyance, frustration or anger — can keep you from becoming part of the problem.

Find Alternative Paths
to Success

SOMETIMES AN ASSHOLE feels like more than an asshole. They feel like a roadblock on the way toward office success for you. And that may well be the truth. If that block can't be moved out of your way, it's incumbent upon you to find another path around it. Is there a way that the workflow can work around this jerk? Can you get yourself reassigned? Will additional education help carve a new path?

Office Yoga

WHETHER YOU'RE A contractor working on a new building or an office drone strapped to your desk for hours, the added aggravation of an office asshole can magnify the knots in your back, the crick in your neck and the ache behind your eyes. A bit of office yoga could help. A few clicks of your mouse will lead you to yoga moves that will help avoid "tech neck," stretch out your legs, or loosen up your shoulders. But yoga isn't just exercise. It's a set of simple, disciplined moves designed for both health and relaxation.

№ 83

Protect Your Reputation

PREPARING TO FIGHT back against the asshole? Make sure your own ass is covered. As mentioned earlier, make sure your social media history is clean. You don't want a tweet written in anger or an easy-to-misinterpret Facebook post to come back to haunt you. Make sure you have a trail to show your own success with the business. And review who else in the office — or what former employees — may have dirt on you that could show up in the mix when the mud starts flying.

Feel Better by Holding the Awful Office Film Festival

NO, WE SHOULDN'T take pleasure in someone else's misery. But if that misery is cinematic and not real, why not enjoy characters who have it worse than you? And there seems to be a good one from every generation, whether it's 1980's *Nine to Five*, 1988's *Working Girl*, 1992's *Glengarry Glen Ross*, or, for the firing sequence alone, 2009's *Up in the Air*. And then, of course, there's the *Citizen Kane* of the office hell genre, *Office Space*.

Visualization

CAN'T PHYSICALLY ESCAPE from the workplace? How about a quick trip to your happy place? Close your eyes (assuming you aren't operating heavy machinery or driving a vehicle of any kind) and imagine that you are at the place where you are happiest. Think about the smells, the sounds, what you see and what you feel. Such a mental vacation may not earn frequent flier points, but it can be a getaway that helps get you through the day.

Beware of Addictive Escapes

IT'S UNLIKELY ANYONE but the most hardcore teetotaler would begrudge you a drink after an especially bad day at the office. But be careful not to use the office asshole's behavior as an excuse to indulge in drink or drugs on a regular basis, lest you create a problem far bigger than the one making your workplace toxic.

Better Yourself

RATHER THAN FOCUS attention on bringing down the office asshole, look for ways to improve yourself. Are there online classes in your field? Sites that will help you pick up new skills? A nearby university or trade school that could up your importance to your company? Remember that the better you look, the worse they look.

Search for the Win-Win

WHILE THE SITUATION may feel adversarial, it doesn't have to be you versus them. Is there something the asshole seems to want — or is obviously stating that they want? Rather than try to make sure they don't get it, think about whether there's a win-win scenario where you both get what you want.

№ 89

Perform Random Acts
of Kindness

THIS IS NOT to suggest that you bring a fruit basket to the asshole. Or even a box of donuts. No, these random acts of kindness are to help others while also helping you feel better about yourself and your place in the workplace universe. Send a thank-you note (not an e-mail) to a person that helped you. Put in a good word for a hardworking coworker. Pick up that trash in the corner that everyone's ignoring. In the process, you create not only a more positive workspace, but also a more positive mental outlook for yourself.

№ 90

Stay Focused

REMIND YOURSELF WHY you were hired. Remind yourself of the positive comments made at your last performance review. Remind yourself of the things you've done recently to make your workplace a better place to work. And then make a list of the things you can do to make this review even better and to upgrade your workplace even more.

Nº 91

Accept the Imbalance of Power

A SAD TRUTH of some situations is that some people have more power in the workplace than others. That's the nature of the game. And sometimes the asshole is in a position of greater power than you. Understanding where power lies will not only help you avoid a situation where the asshole wields power in a way that costs you your job, it also could help you figure out how to gain the influence of those more powerful than them.

Meditate

YES, YOGA HAS already been mentioned. But not all mind/body/wellness efforts are the same. When the asshole energy is really bad, having a few mindfulness exercises at your disposal may not impact the jerk, but they could help you get through a particularly difficult shift. And they don't require you to get in a "what the heck are they doing?" position.

Synchronized Breathing

IT'S EASY FOR someone to say "Take a deep breath." It's not always easy, though, to actually take that advice. That's why Apple and other companies have created breathing apps that guide you toward slow, intentional breathing. The goal: Clear your head, help you focus, and keep you from doing something you'll really, really regret.

Appear Crazy

NOTHING MAKES PEOPLE uneasy like the belief that there's something "off" about the person that they're messing with. It's important to remember, though, that the ONLY person you act crazy around is your asshole tormentor. And it has to be nebulous — stuff that would be taken as weird but nonthreatening by a third party (say, someone in HR) but would seem infinitely darker to someone who was actively messing with your shit. True assholes also tend to be a bit paranoid, so a little bit of this could go a long way.

Plant Your Plants

INDOOR PLANTS MAY reduce psychological stress, so turning your office space into a mini-Amazonian rain forest could help make it easier for you to manage the tension created by the presence of a workplace asshole. Go green.

Silence

THERE'S A DIFFERENCE between ignoring a problem — which is often a very bad idea — and willfully using silence as a weapon to fight back against assholery. An asshole often doesn't know what to do with silence — they feed off feedback, thrive off engagement. A stare and a grin can go a long way.

Have Encounter Exit Strategies

WHEN YOU'VE GOT a meeting scheduled that you know will involve the asshole, make sure to have a place you need to be immediately after. The more lingering moments you have, the greater the potential for awkward power plays. Timing things so that you aren't riding the elevator or walking through the parking garage with the asshole are also highly recommended.

Assess the Asshole's Genius

IT'S CLICHÉ, BUT some clichés are anchored in truth: Asshole behavior is often linked with genius. Or, at least, with people so focused on achievement and locked into their thinking that they aren't aware of their impact on other people. Sometimes, bosses can value a biggie-sized brain — even with accompanying asshole behavior — over the downside they might create. And sometimes that can help you build up tolerance.

Don't Take the Blame

OFFICE ASSHOLES OFTEN target the weak spots in the workforce. Don't let that be you. When they try to pin the blame on you for their own mistakes or use you to lighten their own workload, stand up to it. Once you start letting yourself get walked on, you become the recurring doormat. The longer such actions fester, the more you seem to be the problem.

Fire Them

OF COURSE, THE best thing you can do, if you are in the position to do so, is to fire the asshole. If you can't do that right now, then working your way into a position of responsibility — or chumming up to those who are — could be a long-term plan that helps you get through the day. If not, just fantasize about that moment the way Eliza Doolittle fantasizes about extracting vengeance on Henry Higgins in *My Fair Lady*.

Use the Asshole
as Motivation

LET'S SPIN THIS to the positive: An office asshole may be the fuel you need to propel yourself to the next level. You're better than that jerk, right? You're more important to the business than that jerk, right? Well, take their behavior as an opportunity to prove it. Success can be the best revenge.

Good luck!

To tolerate working with an asshole, you'll need it.

*About the
Author*

LOU HARRY IS the author of more than 30 books including *Office Dares*, *The High-Impact Infidelity Diet; A Novel*, and *Kid Culture*. While Lou doesn't have any assholes at his current workplace, he's got plenty of stories about assholes he's worked with in the past, including E.K., S.F., and R.B., to initial just a few.

Find him at www.louharry.com or by tweeting @LouHarry.

About the
Illustrator

ALEX KALOMERIS IS an illustrator, animator, printmaker, and all around storyteller. His work revolves around creating narratives, characters, and impressions. Nautical, natural, and nostalgic themes show up in his work and are an integral part of his identity as an artist. If he cannot be found in his studio, he is probably out wandering the forests and hills of his home.

Find him online at www.alexkalomeris.com.

ABOUT CIDER MILL PRESS BOOK PUBLISHERS

Good ideas ripen with time. From seed to harvest, Cider Mill Press brings fine reading, information, and entertainment together between the covers of its creatively crafted books. Our Cider Mill bears fruit twice a year, publishing a new crop of titles each spring and fall.

"Where Good Books Are Ready for Press"

Visit us on the web at
www.cidermillpress.com
or write to us at
PO Box 454
12 Spring St.
Kennebunkport, Maine 04046